If found, please return to

_____

_____

_____

_____

_____

The
Cambridge
Pocket Diary

2019–2020

The
Cambridge
Pocket Diary

2019–2020

CAMBRIDGE
UNIVERSITY PRESS

University Printing House, Cambridge CB2 8BS, United Kingdom

Cambridge University Press is part of the University of Cambridge.

It furthers the University's mission by disseminating knowledge in the pursuit of education, learning and research at the highest international levels of excellence.

www.cambridge.org
Information on this title: www.cambridge.org/978-1-108-70870-8

First published 2019

Printed in the United Kingdom by FLB Group Ltd

ISBN 978-1-108-70870-8

CONTENTS

2019	S	M	Tu	W	Th	F	S
Oct.	...	...	1	2	3	4	5
	6	7	[8	9	10	11	1
	13	14	15	16	17	18	1
	20	21	22	23	24	25	2
	27	28	29	30	31	...	..
Nov.	...	...	...	...	...	1	2
	3	4	5	6	7	8	9
	10	11	12	13	14	15	1
	17	18	19	20	21	22	2
	24	25	26	27	28	29	3
Dec.	1	2	3	4	5	6]	7
	8	9	10	11	12	13	1
	15	16	17	18	19	*20*	*2*
	22	*23*	*24*	*25*	*26**	*27*	*2*
	29	*30*	*31*	...	...	..	
2020							
Jan.	...	...	...	1*	2	3	4
	5	6	7	8	9	10	1
	12	13	[14	15	16	17	1
	19	20	21	22	23	24	2
	26	27	28	29	30	31	...
Feb.	...	...	...	...	...	...	1
	2	3	4	5	6	7	8
	9	10	11	12	13	14	1
	16	17	18	19	20	21	2
	23	24	25	26	27	28	2
Mar.	1	2	3	4	5	6	7
	8	9	10	11	12	13]	1
	15	16	17	18	19	20	2
	22	23	24	*25*	*26*	*27*	*28*
	29	*30*	*31*	...	...	...	

Vacations are shown by italic figures. First and period of residence are shown by square brackets

THE YEAR 2019–20

2020	S	M	Tu	W	Th	F	S
APR.	...	...	...	1	2	3	4
	5	6	7	8	9	**10**	**11**
	12	**13***	**14**	**15**	**16**	**17**	**18**
	19	**20**	[**21**	**22**	**23**	**24**	**25**
	26	**27**	**28**	**29**	**30**	...	...
MAY	...	...	...	...	...	**1**	**2**
	3	**4**	**5**	**6**	**7**	**8***	**9**
	10	**11**	**12**	**13**	**14**	**15**	**16**
	17	**18**	**19**	**20**	**21**	**22**	**23**
	24	**25***	**26**	**27**	**28**	**29**	**30**
	31	...	...	...	...	...	...
UNE	...	**1**	**2**	**3**	**4**	**5**	**6**
	7	**8**	**9**	**10**	**11**	**12**]	**13**
	14	**15**	**16**	**17**	**18**	19	20
	21	22	23	24	25	26	27
	28	29	30	...	...	...	...
JULY	...	...	...	1	2	3	4
	5	[6	7	8	9	10	11
	12	13	14	15	16	17	18
	19	20	21	22	23	24	25
	26	27	28	29	30	31	...
AUG.	...	...	...	...	...	...	1
	2	3	4	5	6	7	8]
	9	10	11	12	13	14	15
	16	17	18	19	20	21	22
	23	24	25	26	27	28	29
	30	31*	...	...	...	...	...
EP.	...	...	1	2	3	4	5
	6	7	8	9	10	11	12
	13	14	15	16	17	18	19
	20	21	22	23	24	25	26
	27	28	29	30	...	...	...

st days of Full Term and of the Long Vacation
n asterisk denotes a Bank Holiday.

MICHAELMAS TERM LECTURE-LIST

	Monday	Tuesday	Wednesday	Thursday	Friday	Saturday
9.0–10.0						
10.0–11.0						
11.0–12.0						
12.0–1.0						
1.0–2.0						

2.0–3.0					
3.0–4.0					
4.0–5.0					
5.0–6.0					
6.0–7.0					

LENT TERM LECTURE-LIST

	Monday	Tuesday	Wednesday	Thursday	Friday	Saturday
9.0–10.0						
10.0–11.0						
11.0–12.0						
12.0–1.0						
1.0–2.0						

2.0–3.0				
3.0–4.0				
4.0–5.0				
5.0–6.0				
6.0–7.0				

EASTER TERM LECTURE-LIST

	Monday	Tuesday	Wednesday	Thursday	Friday	Saturday
9.0–10.0						
10.0–11.0						
11.0–12.0						
12.0–1.0						
1.0–2.0						

2.0–3.0					
3.0–4.0					
4.0–5.0					
5.0–6.0					
6.0–7.0					

S
1

ELEVENTH SUNDAY AFTER TRINITY
Al Hijra (Islamic)
Sun rises 6.10, sets 7.48

M
2

Tu
3

Research Period

W
4

Th
5

F
6

Moon's First Quarter, 3.10 a.m.
Press Syndicate (Academic Publishing Committee), 2.15

S
7

Research Period

S
8

TWELFTH SUNDAY AFTER TRINITY
Sun rises 6.22, sets 7.32

M
9

Tu
10

Research Period

W
11

Th
12

Press & Assessment Board, 1.0

F
13

S
14

Full Moon, 4.33 a.m.

Research Period

S
15

THIRTEENTH SUNDAY AFTER TRINITY
Sun rises 6.33, sets 7.15
Duke of Sussex born, 1984

M
16

Tu
17

**W
18**

**Th
19**

**F
20**

VIGIL

**S
21**

ST MATTHEW

SEPTEMBER 2019

S
22

FOURTEENTH SUNDAY AFTER TRINITY
Moon's Last Quarter, 2.41 a.m.
Sun rises 6.45, sets 6.59

M
23

Council, 10.15

Tu
24

Research Period

W
25

Th
26

F
27

Press Syndicate (Academic Publishing Committee), 2.15
Alumni Festival begins

S
28

New Moon, 6.26 p.m.

Research Period

S 29

FIFTEENTH SUNDAY AFTER TRINITY
ST MICHAEL AND ALL ANGELS
Rosh HaShanah (Jewish) begins
Navarathri (Hindu) begins
Sun rises 6.56, sets 6.42
Alumni Festival ends

M 30

Fitzwilliam Museum Syndicate, 2.15

Tu 1

MICHAELMAS TERM begins
Congregation of the Regent House (Vice-Chancellor's
Address & election and admission of Proctors), 9.30
Press & Assessment Board, 1.0

Michaelmas Term

W 2

Finance Committee of the Council, 10.15
General Board, 2.0

Th 3

Audit Committee, 10.15

F 4

S 5

Moon's First Quarter, 4.47 p.m.

Michaelmas Term

S 6

SIXTEENTH SUNDAY AFTER TRINITY
Sun rises 7.8, sets 6.26

M 7

Dussehra (Hindu)
Board of Engineering, 2.15
Antiquarian Society, 6.0

Tu 8

FULL TERM begins
Board of Business & Management, 2.15
Council of School of Clinical Medicine, 10.0
Discussion, 2.0

W 9

St Denys
Yom Kippur (Jewish)

Th 10

Board of Education, 3.30
Board of Law, 2.30
Board of Veterinary Medicine, 1.0

F 11

Press Syndicate (Academic Publishing Committee), 2.1

S 12

S

13

SEVENTEENTH SUNDAY AFTER TRINITY
Full Moon, 9.8 p.m.
Sun rises 7.20, sets 6.10
Oxford Full Term begins

M

14

Council, 10, 15
Board of History & Philosophy of Science, 2.30
Board of Modern & Medieval Languages &
    Linguistics, 1.45
Board of Philosophy, 2.0

Tu

15

Board of Architecture & History of Art, 1.45
Board of Asian & Middle Eastern Studies, 2.0
Board of Clinical Medicine, 10.0
Board of Computer Science & Technology, 2.15
Board of History, 2.15
Development Studies Committee, 1.0
Natural Sciences Tripos Committee, 2.15
Library Syndicate, 2.0

Michaelmas Term

W
16

Th
17

St Etheldreda
Board of Divinity, 2.15
Board of Human, Social, & Political Science, 2.0
Board of Music, 2.15

F
18

ST LUKE

S
19

Michaelmas Term

S
20

EIGHTEENTH SUNDAY AFTER TRINITY
Sun rises 7.33, sets 5.55
Preacher, Rev. N.G.P. Gumbel, *T*, Vicar of Holy Trinity,
Brompton, 11.15
End of first quarter of Michaelmas Term

M
21

Simchat Torah (Jewish)
Moon's Last Quarter, 12.39 p.m.
Board of Biology , 4.15
Board of Economics, 2.0
Philosophical Society Council (and A.G.M.), 4.45

Tu
22

Board of Earth Sciences & Geography, 2.15
Council of School of Arts & Humanities, 2.0
Discussion, 2.0

Michaelmas Term

W 23

Th 24
United Nations Day
Board of Classics, 2.0
Board of Mathematics, 2.15
Bursars' Committee, 2.15
Colleges' Committee, 10.0
Council of School of Physical Sciences, 10.0

F 25
Board of Physics & Chemistry, 2.15
Senior Tutors' Committee, 2.15
Council of School of Humanities & Social Sciences, 2.0
Council of School of Technology, 2.0
Press Syndicate (Academic Publishing Committee), 2.1

S 26
VIGIL
Congregation of the Regent House, 11.0

Michaelmas Term

S 27

NINETEENTH SUNDAY AFTER TRINITY
Diwali (Hindu)
Bandi Chhor Divas (Sikh)
Sun rises 6.45, sets 4.41
Summer Time ends

M 28

ST SIMON AND ST JUDE
New Moon, 3.38 a.m.
Council of School of Biological Sciences, 2.0

Tu 29

Michaelmas Term

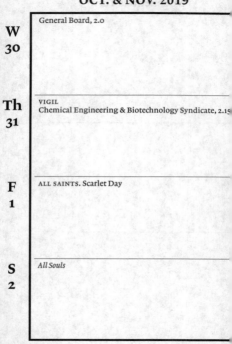

W
30

General Board, 2.0

Th
31

VIGIL
Chemical Engineering & Biotechnology Syndicate, 2.15

F
1

ALL SAINTS. Scarlet Day

S
2

All Souls

Michaelmas Term

S
3

TWENTIETH SUNDAY AFTER TRINITY
Sun rises 6.58, sets 4.28
Commemoration of Benefactors. Scarlet Day.
  Preacher, Rev. S.R.I. Foot, *CAI*, Regius Professor of
  Ecclesiastical History & Canon Professor of Christ
  Church in the University of Oxford (*Lady Margaret's
  Preacher*), 11.15

M
4

Moon's First Quarter, 10.23 a.m.
Antiquarian Society, 6.0

Tu
5

Press & Assessment Board, 1.0
Discussion, 2.0

Michaelmas Term

W 6

Roll of the Regent House and Lists of Faculties promulgated
Faculty of Veterinary Medicine, Annual Meeting, 1.0

Th 7

Board of Divinity, 2.15
Board of Law, 2.15
Smuts Fund Managers, 2.30

F 8

Press Syndicate (Academic Publishing Committee), 2.15

S 9

Michaelmas Term divides

S
10

TWENTY-FIRST SUNDAY AFTER TRINITY
Remembrance Sunday
Sun rises 7.12, sets 4.16

M
11

Board of Clinical Medicine, and Annual Meeting of the
    Faculty, 1.0
Local Examinations Syndicate, 1.30
Press Syndicate, 11.0

Tu
12

Guru Nanak Birthday (Sikh)
Full Moon, 1.34 p.m.
Board of Computer Science & Technology, and Annual
    Meeting of the Faculty, 2.15
University & Assistants Joint Board, 2.15

W 13

Finance Committee of the Council, 10.15
Botanic Garden Syndicate, 2.15

Th 14

Prince of Wales born, 1948
Faculty of Classics, Annual Meeting, 9.0
Faculty of Law, Annual Meeting, 1.0

F 15

Nativity Fast (Orthodox) begins

S 16

S
17

TWENTY-SECOND SUNDAY AFTER TRINITY
Sun rises 7.23, sets 4.5

M
18

Audit Committee, 10.15
Board of Engineering, 2.15
Board of History & Philosophy of Science, 2.30
Board of Philosophy, 2.0
Philosophical Society Council, 4.45

Tu
19

Moon's Last Quarter, 9.11 p.m.
Board of Architecture & History of Art, and Annual
  Meeting of the Faculty, 1.45
Board of Asian & Middle Eastern Studies, and Annual
  Meeting of the Faculty, 2.0
Board of Business & Management, 2.15
Board of Earth Sciences & Geography, and Annual
  Meeting of the Faculty, 2.15
Faculty of History, Annual Meeting, 2.15
Discussion, 2.0

W 20

St Edmund

Th 21

Board of Education, 3.30
Board of Mathematics, and Annual Meeting of the
    Faculty, 2.15
Board of Music, and Annual Meeting of the Faculty, 2.15
Board of Veterinary Medicine, 1.0
Council of School of Physical Sciences, 10.0

F 22

St Cecilia
Board of Physics & Chemistry, 2.15
Senior Tutors' Committee, 2.15
Press Syndicate (Academic Publishing Committee), 2.15

S 23

Antiquarian Society Conference, 10.0

Michaelmas Term

S
24

TWENTY-THIRD SUNDAY AFTER TRINITY
Sun rises 7.35, sets 3.57

M
25

St Catharine of Alexandria
Council, 10.15
Board of Economics, 2.0
Board of Modern & Medieval Languages & Linguistics, 1.4
Council of School of Biological Sciences, 2.0
Fitzwilliam Museum Syndicate, 2.15

Tu
26

New Moon, 3.6 p.m.
Board of Computer Science & Technology, 2.15
Board of History, 2.15
Natural Sciences Tripos Committee, 2.15
Council of School of Arts & Humanities, 2.0
Council of School of Clinical Medicine, 2.0

W
27

General Board, 2.0

Th
28

Board of Human, Social, & Political Science, 3.0, and
Annual Meeting of the Faculty, 2.0
Accommodation Syndicate, 10.0

F
29

VIGIL
Council of School of Technology, 2.0
End of third quarter of Michaelmas Term

S
30

ST ANDREW
Congregation of the Regent House, 2.0

Michaelmas Term

S
1

FIRST SUNDAY IN ADVENT
St Eligius
Sun rises 7.46, sets 3.52

M
2

Antiquarian Society, 6.0

Tu
3

Press & Assessment Board, 2.0
Discussion, 2.0

W 4

Moon's First Quarter, 6.58 a.m.

Th 5

Board of Classics, 2.0
Board of Divinity, 2.15
Board of Law, 2.15

F 6

St Nicholas
Council of School of Humanities & Social Sciences, 2.0
FULL TERM ends

S 7

Oxford Full Term ends

S 8

SECOND SUNDAY IN ADVENT
Sun rises 7.55, sets 3.48

M 9

Council, 10.15

Tu 10

Michaelmas Term

W
11

Th
12

Full Moon, 5.12 a.m.

F
13

S
14

Michaelmas Term

S
15

THIRD SUNDAY IN ADVENT
Sun rises 8.2, sets 3.47

M
16

O Sapientia

Tu
17

Michaelmas Term

W
18

Th
19

Moon's Last Quarter, 4.57 a.m.
MICHAELMAS TERM ends

F
20

VIGIL

S
21

ST THOMAS

Michaelmas Term

S
22

FOURTH SUNDAY IN ADVENT
Chanukkah (Jewish)
Sun rises 8.7, sets 3.49

M
23

Tu
24

VIGIL
Library closed

Christmas Vacation

W
25

CHRISTMAS DAY. Scarlet Day
Library closed

Th
26

ST STEPHEN
New Moon, 5.13 a.m.
Bank Holiday
Library closed

F
27

ST JOHN THE EVANGELIST
Library closed

S
28

INNOCENTS' DAY
Library closed

Christmas Vacation

S
29

SUNDAY AFTER CHRISTMAS
Sun rises 8.9, sets 3.54

M
30

Library closed

Tu
31

Library closed

Christmas Vacation

W 1

CIRCUMCISION
Bank Holiday
Library Closed

Th 2

F 3

Moon's First Quarter, 4.45 a.m.

S 4

Christmas Vacation

S 5

SECOND SUNDAY AFTER CHRISTMAS
Sun rises 8.8, sets 4.2
LENT TERM begins

M 6

EPIPHANY
Antiquarian Society, 6.0

Tu 7

Lent Term

W 8

Finance Committee of the Council, 10.15

Th 9

Duchess of Cambridge born, 1982

F 10

Full Moon, 7.21 p.m.
Press Syndicate (Academic Publishing Committee), 2.15

S 11

Lent Term

S
12

FIRST SUNDAY AFTER EPIPHANY
Sun rises 8.4, sets 4.11

M
13

Tu
14

FULL TERM begins
Board of Business & Management, 2.15

W 15

Makar Sandranti (Hindu)
General Board, 2.0

Th 16

Audit Committee, 10.15
Board of Education, 3.30
Board of Law, 3.0

F 17

Moon's Last Quarter, 12.58 p.m.

S 18

Lent Term

S
19

SECOND SUNDAY AFTER EPIPHANY
Sun rises 7.58, sets 4.22
Oxford Full Term begins

M
20

Council, 10.15
Board of Engineering, 2.15
Board of History & Philosophy of Science, 2.30
Council of School of Biological Sciences, 2.0
Philosophical Society Council, 4.45

Tu
21

Board of Architecture & History of Art, 1.45
Board of Clinical Medicine, 10.0
Board of Computer Science & Technology, 2.15
Board of Earth Sciences & Geography, 2.15
Board of History, 2.15
Development Studies Committee, 1.0
Discussion, 2.0

W
22

Th
23

Board of Divinity, 2.15
Board of Human, Social, & Political Science, 2.0
Board of Mathematics, 2.15

F
24

New Moon, 9.42 p.m.
Board of Physics & Chemistry, 2.15
Press Syndicate (Academic Publishing Committee), 2.1
End of first quarter of Lent Term

S
25

CONVERSION OF ST PAUL
Congregation of the Regent House, 2.0

S 26

THIRD SUNDAY AFTER EPIPHANY
Sun rises 7.50, sets 4.35
Preacher, Prof. P. Ward, Professor of Practical Theology
   in the University of Durham, 11.15

M 27

Board of Economics, 2.0
Board of Philosophy, 2.0
Fitzwilliam Museum Syndicate, 2.15

Tu 28

Natural Sciences Tripos Committee, 2.15
Council of School of Arts & Humanities, 2.0
Council of School of Clinical Medicine, 10.0

Lent Term

W
29

Th
30

Board of Classics, 2.0
Board of Veterinary Medicine, 1.0
Council of School of Physical Sciences, 10.0

F
31

Council of School of Humanities & Social Sciences, 2.0
Council of School of Technology, 2.0

S
1

VIGIL

Lent Term

S
2

FOURTH SUNDAY AFTER EPIPHANY
PURIFICATION OF THE BLESSED VIRGIN MARY
Candlemas
Moon's First Quarter, 1.42 a.m.
Sun rises 7.39, sets 4.48

M
3

Antiquarian Society, 6.0

Tu
4

St Gilbert of Sempringham
Board of Asian & Middle Eastern Studies, 2.0
Press & Assessment Board, 1.0
University & Assistants Joint Board, 2.15
Library Syndicate, 2.0
Discussion, 2.0

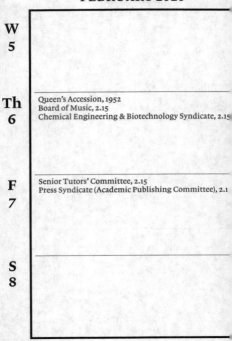

W 5

Th 6
Queen's Accession, 1952
Board of Music, 2.15
Chemical Engineering & Biotechnology Syndicate, 2.15

F 7
Senior Tutors' Committee, 2.15
Press Syndicate (Academic Publishing Committee), 2.1

S 8

Lent Term

S 9

SEPTUAGESIMA SUNDAY
Full Moon, 7.33 a.m.
Sun rises 7.27, sets 5.1

M 10

St Scholastica
Board of Biology, 4.15
Board of Modern & Medieval Languages &
    Linguistics, 1.45

Tu 11

St Radegund

W
12

General Board, 2.0
Botanic Garden Syndicate, 2.15

Th
13

Board of Divinity, 2.15
Board of Law, 2.15
Bursars' Committee, 2.15
Colleges' Committee, 10.0
Smuts Fund Managers, 2.30
Lent Term divides

F
14

St Valentine

S
15

Moon's Last Quarter, 10.17 p.m.

Lent Term

S 16

SEXAGESIMA SUNDAY
Sun rises 7.14, sets 5.14

M 17

Tu 18

Board of Earth Sciences & Geography, 2.15
Discussion, 2.0

Lent Term

W
19

Duke of York born, 1960

Th
20

Board of Classics, 2.0
Board of Mathematics, 2.15

F
21

Maha Shivrathri (Hindu)
Board of Physics & Chemistry, 2.15
Press Syndicate (Academic Publishing Committee), 2.15

S
22

Congregation of the Regent House, 2.0

FEBRUARY 2020

S 23

QUINQUAGESIMA SUNDAY
New Moon, 3.32 p.m.
Sun rises 7.0, sets 5.27
Preacher, Prof. R. Langton, N, Knightbridge Professor o
   Philosophy (*Hulsean Preacher*), 11.15

M 24

ST MATTHIAS
Council, 10.15
Board of Economics, 2.0

Tu 25

Shrove Tuesday
Board of Asian & Middle Eastern Studies, 2.0
Natural Sciences Tripos Committee, 2.15

W 26

FIRST DAY OF LENT
Ash Wednesday

Th 27

Council of School of Physical Sciences, 10.0

F 28

S 29

Lent Term

S
1

FIRST SUNDAY IN LENT
St David
Sun rises 6.45, sets 5.40

M
2

Great Lent (Orthodox) begins
Moon's First Quarter, 7.57 p.m.
Board of Engineering, 2.15
Board of History & Philosophy of Science, 2.30
Board of Philosophy, 2.0
Antiquarian Society, 6.0
Philosophical Society Council, 4.45

Tu
3

Board of Computer Science & Technology, 2.15
Discussion, 2.0

MARCH 2020

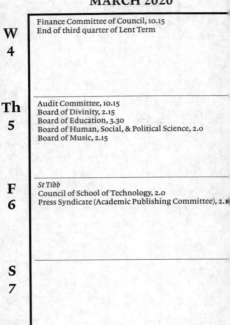

W 4
Finance Committee of Council, 10.15
End of third quarter of Lent Term

Th 5
Audit Committee, 10.15
Board of Divinity, 2.15
Board of Education, 3.30
Board of Human, Social, & Political Science, 2.0
Board of Music, 2.15

F 6
St Tibb
Council of School of Technology, 2.0
Press Syndicate (Academic Publishing Committee), 2.

S 7

S 8

SECOND SUNDAY IN LENT
Sun rises 6.29, sets 5.52

M 9

Full Moon, 5.48 p.m.
Commonwealth Day
Board of Modern & Medieval Languages &
Linguistics, 1.45

Tu 10

Holi (Hindu)
Hola Mohalla (Sikh)
Earl of Wessex born, 1964
Board of Architecture & History of Art, 1.45
Board of Business & Management, 2.15
Board of Earth Sciences & Geography, 2.15
Board of History, 2.15
Press & Assessment Board, 1.0
Council of School of Arts & Humanities, 2.0
Council of School of Clinical Medicine, 2.0

Lent Term

MARCH 2020

W
11

General Board, 2.0

Th
12

Board of Classics, 2.0
Board of Law, 2.15
Board of Veterinary Medicine, 1.0

F
13

Board of Physics & Chemistry, 2.15
Senior Tutors' Committee, 2.15
Council of School of Humanities & Social Sciences, 2.0
FULL TERM ends

S
14

Oxford Full Term ends

S
15

THIRD SUNDAY IN LENT
Sun rises 6.13, sets 6.5

M
16

Moon's Last Quarter, 9.34 a.m.
Council, 10.15
Board of Clinical Medicine, 2.0
Council of School of Biological Sciences, 2.0

Tu
17

St Patrick
Discussion, 2.0

Lent Term

W 18

St Edward, King & Martyr
Accommodation Syndicate, 10.0

Th 19

F 20

Purim (Jewish)
Press Syndicate (Academic Publishing Committee), 2.

S 21

St Benedict
Congregation of the Regent House, 11.0

Lent Term

MARCH 2020

S
22

FOURTH SUNDAY IN LENT
Sun rises 5.57, sets 6.17

M
23

Tu
24

VIGIL
New Moon, 9.28 a.m.
LENT TERM ends

Lent Term

W
25

ANNUNCIATION OF THE BLESSED VIRGIN MARY,
or Lady Day

Th
26

F
27

S
28

Congregation of the Regent House, 11.0

Easter Vacation

S
29

FIFTH SUNDAY IN LENT
Passion Sunday
Sun rises 6.40, sets 7.29
Summer Time begins

M
30

Tu
31

Easter Vacation

W 1

Moon's First Quarter, 10.21 a.m.

Th 2

F 3

S 4

Easter Vacation

S
5

SUNDAY BEFORE EASTER
Palm Sunday
Sun rises 6.24, sets 7.41

M
6

Antiquarian Society (& A.G.M.), 5.54

Tu
7

Easter Vacation

W 8

Full Moon, 2.35 a.m.

Th 9

Maundy Thursday
Pesach (Jewish) begins

F 10

GOOD FRIDAY
Library closed
EASTER TERM begins

S 11

EASTER EVE
VIGIL
Library closed

Easter Term

S
12

EASTER SUNDAY. Scarlet Day
Sun rises 6.8, sets 7.53

M
13

MONDAY IN EASTER WEEK
Bank Holiday
Library closed

Tu
14

Vaisakhi (Sikh)
Moon's Last Quarter, 10.56 p.m.

Easter Term

W
15

Th
16

F
17

S
18

S
19

FIRST SUNDAY AFTER EASTER
Sun rises 5.53, sets 8.5

M
20

Council, 10.15

Tu
21

Queen Elizabeth II born, 1926
FULL TERM begins
Board of Earth Sciences & Geography, 2.15
Mere's Commemoration. Preacher, to be announced, 11.45

W
22

Th
23

St George
New Moon, 2.26 a.m.
Prince Louis of Cambridge born, 2018
Board of Law, 3.0

F
24

Ramadan begins
Press Syndicate (Academic Publishing Committee),
2.15

S
25

ST MARK
Congregation of the Regent House, 11.0

S
26

SECOND SUNDAY AFTER EASTER
Sun rises 5.38, sets 8.17
Oxford Full Term begins

M
27

Board of Modern & Medieval Languages &
  Linguistics, 1.45
Fitzwilliam Museum Syndicate, 2.15
End of first quarter of Easter Term

Tu
28

Board of Business & Management, 2.15
Board of Computer Science & Technology, 2.15
Board of History, 2.15
Press & Assessment Board, 1.0
Council of School of Clinical Medicine, 10.0
Discussion, 2.0

Easter Term

W
29

Finance Committee of Council, 10.15
General Board, 2.0

Th
30

Buddha Day
Moon's First Quarter, 8.38 p.m.
Board of Classics, 2.0
Board of Divinity, 2.15
Board of Mathematics, 2.15

F
1

ST PHILIP AND ST JAMES

S
2

Princess Charlotte of Cambridge born, 2015

Easter Term

S
3

THIRD SUNDAY AFTER EASTER
Sun rises 5.25, sets 8.29

M
4

Tu
5

Board of Asian & Middle Eastern Studies, 2.0
Board of Clinical Medicine, 10.0
Development Studies Committee, 1.0
Natural Sciences Tripos Committee, 2.15
Library Syndicate, 2.0

Easter Term

W 6

St John Evang. ante Portam Latinam

Th 7

Full Moon, 10.45 a.m.
Audit Committee, 10.15
Board of Education, 3.30
Board of Human, Social, & Political Science, 2.0
Board of Veterinary Medicine, 1.0
Council of School of Physical Sciences, 10.0
Philological Society (A.G.M.), 4.30

F 8

Bank Holiday (V.E. Day Anniversary).
Senior Tutors' Committee, 2.15
Council of School of Humanities & Social Sciences, 2.0
Council of School of Technology, 2.0

S 9

S
10

FOURTH SUNDAY AFTER EASTER
Sun rises 5.12, sets 8.41

M
11

Board of Economics, 2.0
Board of Engineering, 2.15
Board of History & Philosophy of Science, 2.30
Antiquarian Society, 6.0
Philosophical Society Council, 4.45

Tu
12

Lag ba – Omer (Jewish)
Council of School of Arts & Humanities, 2.0
Discussion, 2.0

W 13
Botanic Garden Syndicate, 2.15
Local Examinations Syndicate, 1.30
Press Syndicate, 11.0

Th 14
Moon's Last Quarter, 2.3 p.m.
Board of Law, 2.15
Board of Music, 2.15
Chemical Engineering & Biotechnology Syndicate, 2.1
Smuts Fund Managers, 2.30
Easter Term divides

F 15

S 16
Congregation of the Regent House, 10.0

S
17

FIFTH SUNDAY AFTER EASTER
Rogation Sunday
Sun rises 5.1, sets 8.52

M
18

Council, 10.15
Board of Philosophy, 2.0
Council of School of Biological Sciences, 2.0

Tu
19

Board of Architecture & History of Art, 1.45
Board of Earth Sciences & Geography, 2.15

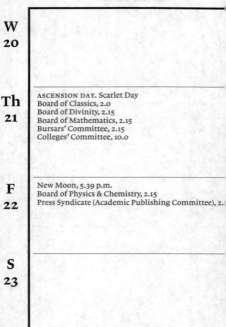

W
20

Th
21

ASCENSION DAY. Scarlet Day
Board of Classics, 2.0
Board of Divinity, 2.15
Board of Mathematics, 2.15
Bursars' Committee, 2.15
Colleges' Committee, 10.0

F
22

New Moon, 5.39 p.m.
Board of Physics & Chemistry, 2.15
Press Syndicate (Academic Publishing Committee), 2.

S
23

S
24

SUNDAY AFTER ASCENSION DAY
Eid ul-Fitr (Islamic)
Sun rises 4.52, sets 9.2

M
25

Bank Holiday

Tu
26

Discussion, 2.0

W
27

The Venerable Bede

Th
28

F
29

Shavuot (Jewish) begins

S
30

Moon's First Quarter, 3.30 a.m.

S
31

WHITSUNDAY. Scarlet Day
Sun rises 4.45, sets 9.10
Preacher, M.G. Carcaño, Resident Bishop of the San
   Francisco Area, California– Nevada Conference
of the United Methodist Church (*Ramsden Preacher*), 11.1

M
1

End of third quarter of Easter Term

Tu
2

Coronation of Queen Elizabeth II, 1953
Board of Asian & Middle Eastern Studies, 2.0
Board of Business & Management, 2.15
Press & Assessment Board, 1.0
Council of School of Clinical Medicine, 2.0

JUNE 2020

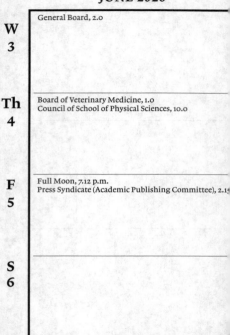

W 3

General Board, 2.0

Th 4

Board of Veterinary Medicine, 1.0
Council of School of Physical Sciences, 10.0

F 5

Full Moon, 7.12 p.m.
Press Syndicate (Academic Publishing Committee), 2.15

S 6

Easter Term

S 7

TRINITY SUNDAY. Scarlet Day
Sun rises 4.40, sets 9.17

M 8

Board of Biology, 4.15
Board of Clinical Medicine, 2.0
Board of Economics, 2.0

Tu 9

Board of Earth Sciences & Geography, 2.15
University & Assistants Joint Board, 2.15
Discussion, 2.0

JUNE 2020

W 10

Duke of Edinburgh born, 1921

Th 11

ST BARNABAS
Corpus Christi
Board of Human, Social, & Political Science, 2.0

F 12

Board of Physics & Chemistry, 2.15
Council of School of Humanities & Social Sciences, 2.0
Council of School of Technology, 2.0
FULL TERM ends

S 13

Moon's Last Quarter, 6.24 a.m.
Queen's Official Birthday (to be confirmed)

S
14

FIRST SUNDAY AFTER TRINITY
Sun rises 4.38, sets 9.22

M
15

Council, 10.15
Board of Engineering, 2.15

Tu
16

Board of History, 2.15
Council of School of Arts & Humanities, 2.0

JUNE 2020

W 17

St Botolph
Accommodation Syndicate, 10.0
Congregation of the Regent House (Honorary Degrees)
  2.45

Th 18

Board of Music, 2.15
EASTER TERM ends

F 19

S 20

Oxford Full Term ends

S 21

SECOND SUNDAY AFTER TRINITY
New Moon, 6.41 a.m.
Duke of Cambridge born, 1982
Sun rises 4.38, sets 9.25

M 22

Board of Modern & Medieval Languages & Linguistics, 1.45

Tu 23

Board of Law, 2.15

Research Period

JUNE 2020

W 24
ST JOHN BAPTIST
Midsummer
Congregations of the Regent House
(General Admission)
Scarlet Day

Th 25
Congregations of the Regent House
(General Admission)
Scarlet Day
Board of Classics, 2.0
Board of Education, 3.30

F 26
Congregations of the Regent House
(General Admission)
Scarlet Day

S 27
Congregations of the Regent House
(General Admission)
Scarlet Day

Research Period

S
28

THIRD SUNDAY AFTER TRINITY
Moon's First Quarter, 8.16 a.m.
Sun rises 4.41, sets 9.24

M
29

ST PETER
Board of History & Philosophy of Science, 2.30
Board of Philosophy, 2.0

Tu
30

Board of Architecture & History of Art, 1.45
Board of Business & Management, 9.30
Board of Classics, 10.0
Board of Computer Science & Technology, 2.15
Council of School of Clinical Medicine, 10.0

W 1

Botanic Garden Syndicate, 2.15

Th 2

Audit Committee, 10.15
Board of Divinity, 2.15

F 3

Press Syndicate (Academic Publishing Committee), 2.1

S 4

S
5

FOURTH SUNDAY AFTER TRINITY
Full Moon, 4.44 a.m.
Sun rises 4.46, sets 9.22

M
6

Board of Engineering, 2.15
Council of School of Biological Sciences, 2.0
Philosophical Society Council, 4.45
Taught summer courses begin not earlier than this day

Tu
7

Natural Sciences Tripos Committee, 2.15
Discussion, 2.0

JULY 2020

W 8

Finance Committee of the Council, 10.15
General Board, 2.0

Th 9

Bursars' Committee, 2.15
Colleges' Committee, 10.0

F 10

Senior Tutors' Committee, 2.15

S 11

Research Period

S 12

FIFTH SUNDAY AFTER TRINITY
Moons' Last Quarter, 11.29 p.m.
Sun rises 4.53, sets 9.16

M 13

Council, 10.15

Tu 14

Press & Assessment Board, 1.0

Research Period

W
15

St Swithin

Th
16

F
17

Duchess of Cornwall born, 1947
Congregation of the Regent House, 10.0

S
18

Congregation of the Regent House, 10.0

Research Period

S
19

SIXTH SUNDAY AFTER TRINITY
Sun rises 5.2, sets 9.9

M
20

New Moon, 5.33 p.m.
Fitzwilliam Museum Syndicate, 2.15

Tu
21

Board of Clinical Medicine, 10.0

Research Period

W
22

St Mary Magdalene
Prince George of Cambridge, born 2013

Th
23

F
24

VIGIL

S
25

ST JAMES

Research Period

S
26

SEVENTH SUNDAY AFTER TRINITY
Sun rises 5.12, sets 8.59

M
27

Moon's First Quarter, 12.33 p.m.

Tu
28

Research Period

W 29

Th 30

F 31

Eid ul – Adha (Islamic)
Press Syndicate (Academic Publishing Committee), 2.15

S 1

Dormition Fast (Orthodox) begins

Research Period

S
2

EIGHTH SUNDAY AFTER TRINITY
Sun rises 5.23, sets 8.48

M
3

Full Moon, 3.59 p.m.

Tu
4

Research Period

W
5

Th
6

F
7

S
8

Taught summer courses end not later than this day

Research Period

AUGUST 2020

S 9

NINTH SUNDAY AFTER TRINITY
Sun rises 5.34, sets 8.35

M 10

Tu 11

Moon's Last Quarter, 4.45 p.m.

Research Period

W
12

Th
13

F
14

S
15

Dormition (Orthodox)
Princess Royal born, 1950

Research Period

S
16
TENTH SUNDAY AFTER TRINITY
Sun rises 5.45, sets 8.21

M
17

Tu
18

Research Period

W 19 New Moon, 2.42 a.m.

Th 20 Al Hijira (Islamic)

F 21

S 22

Research Period

S
23

ELEVENTH SUNDAY AFTER TRINITY
Sun rises 5.57, sets 8.6

M
24

ST BARTHOLOMEW

Tu
25

Moon's First Quarter, 5.58 p.m.

Research Period

W
26

Th
27

F
28

St Augustine of Hippo

S
29

Research Period

S 30

TWELFTH SUNDAY AFTER TRINITY
Sun rises 6.8, sets 7.51

M 31

Bank Holiday
Library closed

Tu 1

Research Period

**W
2**

Full Moon, 5.22 a.m.

**Th
3**

**F
4**

Press Syndicate (Academic Publishing Committee), 2.

**S
5**

Research Period

S 6

THIRTEENTH SUNDAY AFTER TRINITY
Sun rises 6.20, sets 7.35

M 7

Tu 8

W
9

Th
10

Moon's Last Quarter, 9.26 a.m.

F
11

S
12

S
13

FOURTEENTH SUNDAY AFTER TRINITY
Sun rises 6.31, sets 7.18

M
14

Tu
15

Duke of Sussex born, 1984

Research Period

W
16

Th
17

New Moon, 11.0 a.m.
Press & Assessment Board, 1.0

F
18

S
19

Rosh HaShanah (Jewish) begins

S
20

FIFTEENTH SUNDAY AFTER TRINITY
Sun rises 6.43, sets 7.2

M
21

ST MATTHEW
Council, 10.15

Tu
22

W
23

Th
24

Moon's First Quarter, 1.55 a.m.

F
25

Press Syndicate (Academic Publishing Committee), 2.15
Alumni Festival begins

S
26

Research Period

S
27

SIXTEENTH SUNDAY AFTER TRINITY
Sun rises 6.54, sets 6.45
Alumni Festival ends

M
28

Yom Kippur (Jewish)

Tu
29

ST MICHAEL AND ALL ANGELS

Research Period

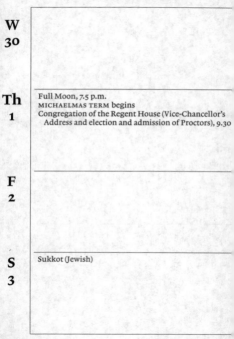

W 30

Th 1
Full Moon, 7.5 p.m.
MICHAELMAS TERM begins
Congregation of the Regent House (Vice-Chancellor's Address and election and admission of Proctors), 9.30

F 2

S 3
Sukkot (Jewish)

Michaelmas Term

S
4

SEVENTEENTH SUNDAY AFTER TRINITY
Sun rises 7.6, sets 6.29

M
5

Tu
6

FULL TERM begins

W
7

Th
8

F
9

St Denys

S
10

Moon's Last Quarter, 12.40 a.m.

S

11

EIGHTEENTH SUNDAY AFTER TRINITY
Simchat Torah (Jewish)
Sun rises 7.18, sets 6.13
Oxford Full Term begins

M

12

Tu

13

W 14

Th 15

F 16

New Moon, 7.31 p.m.

S 17

St Etheldreda
Navaratri (Hindu)

Michaelmas Term

S
18

NINETEENTH SUNDAY AFTER TRINITY
ST LUKE
Sun rises 7.30, sets 5.58

M
19

Tu
20

End of first quarter of Michaelmas Term

W
21

Th
22

F
23

Moon's First Quarter, 1.23 p.m.

S
24

United Nations Day
Congregation of the Regent House, 11.0

Michaelmas Term

S
25

TWENTIETH SUNDAY AFTER TRINITY
Dussehra (Hindu)
Sun rises 6.43, sets 4.43
Summer Time ends

M
26

Tu
27

W
28

ST SIMON AND ST JUDE

Th
29

F
30

S
31

VIGIL
Full Moon, 2.49 p.m.

Michaelmas Term

S
1

TWENTY-FIRST SUNDAY AFTER TRINITY
ALL SAINTS. Scarlet Day
Sun rises 6.56, sets 4.30

All Souls

M
2

Tu
3

W 4

Th 5

F 6 Roll of the Regent House and Lists of Faculties promulgated

S 7

S 8

TWENTY-SECOND SUNDAY AFTER TRINITY
Remembrance Sunday
Moon's Last Quarter, 1.46 p.m.
Sun rises 7.8, sets 4.18

M 9

Michaelmas Term divides

Tu 10

Michaelmas Term

W
11

Th
12

F
13

S
14

Diwali (Hindu)
Prince of Wales born, 1948

Michaelmas Term

S
15

TWENTY-THIRD SUNDAY AFTER TRINITY
Nativity Fast (Orthodox) begins
New Moon, 5.7 a.m.
Sun rises 7.21, sets 4.7

M
16

Tu
17

Michaelmas Term

W
18

Th
19

F
20

St Edmund

S
21

S
22

TWENTY-FOURTH SUNDAY AFTER TRINITY
St Cecilia
Moon's First Quarter, 4.45 a.m.
Sun rises 7.33, sets 3.58

M
23

Tu
24

W
25

St Catharine of Alexandria

Th
26

F
27

S
28

Congregation of the Regent House, 2.0

Michaelmas Term

S
29

FIRST SUNDAY IN ADVENT
Sun rises 7.44, sets 3.52
End of third quarter of Michaelmas Term

M
30

ST ANDREW
Guru Nanak Birthday (Sikh)
Full Moon, 9.30 a.m.

Tu
1

St Eligius

Michaelmas Term

W 2

Th 3

F 4   FULL TERM ends

S 5   Oxford Full Term ends

S
6

SECOND SUNDAY IN ADVENT
St Nicholas
Sun rises 7.53, sets 3.48

M
7

Tu
8

Moon's Last Quarter, 12.37 a.m

Michaelmas Term

W
9

Th
10

F
11

Chanukkah (Jewish)

S
12

Michaelmas Term

S
13

THIRD SUNDAY IN ADVENT
Sun rises 8.1, sets 3.47

M
14

New Moon, 4.17 p.m.

Tu
15

Michaelmas Term

W 16 *O Sapientia*

Th 17

F 18

S 19 MICHAELMAS TERM ends

Michaelmas Term

S
20

FOURTH SUNDAY IN ADVENT
VIGIL
Sun rises 8.6, sets 3.49

M
21

ST THOMAS
Moon's First Quarter, 11.41 p.m

Tu
22

Christmas Vacation

W 23

Th 24
VIGIL
Library closed

F 25
CHRISTMAS Day. Scarlet Day
Library closed

S 26
ST STEPHEN
Library closed

Christmas Vacation

S
27

SUNDAY AFTER CHRISTMAS
ST JOHN THE EVANGELIST
Sun rises 8.9, sets 3.53

M
28

INNOCENTS' DAY
Bank Holiday
Library closed

Tu
29

Library closed

W
30

Full Moon, 3.28 a.m.
Library closed

Th
31

Library closed

Christmas Vacation

Jan.

Feb.

Engagements for MAY

MAY

JUNE

JULY

Aug.

Sept./
Oct.

Nov./
Dec.

AN ALMANAC FO

2020	S	M	Tu	W	Th	F	S
Oct.	...	...	...	...	1	2	3
	4	5	[6	7	8	9	10
	11	12	13	14	15	16	17
	18	19	20	21	22	23	24
	25	26	27	28	29	30	31
Nov.	1	2	3	4	5	6	7
	8	9	10	11	12	13	14
	15	16	17	18	19	20	21
	22	23	24	25	26	27	28
	29	30	...	...	...	...	...
Dec.	...	...	1	2	3	4]	5
	6	7	8	9	10	11	12
	13	14	15	16	17	18	19
	20	*21*	*22*	*23*	*24*	*25*	*26*
	27	28*	29	30	31	...	...
2021 Jan.	...	...	...	...	...	*1**	2
	3	4	5	6	7	8	9
	10	11	12	13	14	15	16
	17	18	[19	20	21	22	23
	24	25	26	27	28	29	30
	31	...	...	...	...	...	...
Feb.	...	1	2	3	4	5	6
	7	8	9	10	11	12	13
	14	15	16	17	18	19	20
	21	22	23	24	25	26	27
	28	...	...	...	...	...	...
Mar.	...	1	2	3	4	5	6
	7	8	9	10	11	12	13
	14	15	16	17	18	19]	20
	21	22	23	24	25	26	27
	28	*29*	*30*	*31*	...	...	...

Vacations are shown by italic figures. First and period of residence are shown by square brackets.

296

THE YEAR 2020–21

2021	S	M	Tu	W	Th	F	S
Apr.	...	...	...	...	1	2	3
	4	5*	6	7	8	9	10
	11	12	13	14	15	16	**17**
	18	**19**	**20**	**21**	**22**	**23**	24
	25	26	[27	**28**	**29**	**30**	
May	...	...	...	...	...	...	**1**
	2	**3***	**4**	**5**	**6**	**7**	**8**
	9	**10**	**11**	**12**	**13**	**14**	**15**
	16	**17**	**18**	**19**	**20**	**21**	**22**
	23	**24**	**25**	**26**	**27**	**28**	**29**
	30	**31***	...	...	...	...	...
June	...	...	**1**	**2**	**3**	**4**	**5**
	6	**7**	**8**	**9**	**10**	**11**	**12**
	13	**14**	**15**	**16**	**17**	**18]**	**19**
	20	**21**	**22**	**23**	**24**	**25**	26
	27	28	29	30	...	...	...
July	...	...	...	...	1	2	3
	4	[5	6	7	8	9	10
	11	12	13	14	15	16	17
	18	19	20	21	22	23	24
	25	26	27	28	29	30	31
Aug.	1	2	3	4	5	6	7]
	8	9	10	11	12	13	14
	15	16	17	18	19	20	21
	22	23	24	25	26	27	28
	29	30*	31	...	...	...	...
Sep.	...	...	...	1	2	3	4
	5	6	7	8	9	10	11
	12	13	14	15	16	17	18
	19	20	21	22	23	24	25
	26	27	28	29	30	...	...

ast days of Full Term and of the Long Vacation
An asterisk denotes a Bank Holiday.

EXAMINATIONS

The Board of Examinations conducts internal Cambridge examinations principally for undergraduates, including those for University scholarships, studentships and prizes. Full current information relating, for example, to guidance to candidates, detailed timetables of examinations (triposes, medical & veterinary, etc.) and of the publication of results, may be found at http://www.admin.cam.ac.uk/students/studentregistry

For information about the admission and examination of graduate students studying for the Ph.D., MSc, M.Litt., and other graduate degrees/qualifications see http://www.admin.cam.ac.uk/offices/gradstud/about

UNIVERSITY OFFICERS

Chancellor Lord SAINSBURY.

Vice-Chancellor Prof. S. J. TOOPE.

Pro-Vice-Chancellors Senior Pro-Vice Chancellor Prof. G. J. VIRGO (Education), Prof. D. CARDWELL (Strategy Planning), Prof. C. ABELL (Research). Prof. A. D. NEEL (Enterprise & Business Relations). Prof. E. V. FERRA (Institutional & International Relations).

High Steward Lord WATSON.

Deputy High Steward A. M. LONSDALE.

Commissary Rt Hon. Lord JUDGE.

Proctors T.K. DICKENS, F. KNIGHTS

Orator R. J. E. THOMPSON.

Registrary E. M. C. RAMPTON, The Old Schools.

Librarian J. P. GARDNER.

Director of the Fitzwilliam Museum and Marlay Curator L. SYSON.

Executive Director of Development & Alumni Relations A. E. TRAUB.

Esquire Bedells N. HARDY, S. V. SCARLETT.

University Advocate Vacant.

Academic Division The Old Schools. *Academic Secretary*: Vacant.

Accommodation Syndicate Kellet Lodge, Tennis Court Road. *Secretary*: N. BLANNING.

Careers Service Stuart House, Mill Lane. *Secretary*: J. C. BLAKESLEY.

Institute of Continuing Education Madingley Hall. *Director*: Prof. J. GAZZARD.

Estate Management Greenwich House, Madingley Road. *Director*: Vacant.

Finance Division The Old Schools. *Director of Finance*: J. D. HUGHES.

Health, Safety and Regulated Facilities Division *Director of Health*: M. VINNELL.

Human Resources Division The Old Schools. *Director*: E. J. STONE.

Local Examinations Syndicate (Cambridge Assessment)
The Triangle Building, Shaftesbury Road. *Group Chief Executive:* S. NASSÉ.

Registry's Office The Old Schools. *Head:* R. B. SACHERS.

Secretaries of Councils of the Schools M. A. BODFISH (*Arts & Humanities*), K. S. DOUGLAS (*Biological Sciences*), C. J. EDMONDS (*Clinical Medicine*), J. G. EVANS (*Humanities & Social Sciences*), J. R. BELLINGHAM (*Physical Sciences*), S. T. LAM (*Technology*).

Sports Centre Philippa Fawcett Drive. *Director of Sport:* N. J. BROOKING.

University Press

Chief Executive of the Press and Secretary of the Press Syndicate:
P. A. J. PHILLIPS.

Director for People: C. ARMOR; *Chief Financial Officer:* A. T. CHANDLER; *Managing Director, ELT:* P. J. COLBERT; *Managing Director, Academic:* A. M-C. HILL; *Chief Information Officer:* M. C. D. MADDOCKS; *General Counsel:* C. A. SHERET; *Managing Director, Education:* R. H. SMITH; *Director of Syndicate Affairs:* K. J. TAYLOR; *Director of Operations:* M. WHITEHOUSE.

UNIVERSITY LIBRARY

For all information about the main University Library see www.lib.cam.ac.uk. For information about affiliated libraries and all other Cambridge libraries, visit the Libraries Gateway at www.lib.cam.ac.uk/camlibraries.

Information about exhibitions at University Library's Milstein Exhibition Centre is available at www.lib.cam.ac.uk/exhibitions.

Information about becoming a Friend of Cambridge University Library is available at www.lib.cam.ac.uk/Friends.

Closure dates (main University Library only)

24 December 2019 – 1 January 2020 inclusive; 10 April – 13 April 2020 inclusive; 31 August 2020, 24 December 2020 – 3 January 2021 inclusive.

Librarian: J. P. GARDNER.

MUSEUMS, ETC.

Fitzwilliam Museum

Open to the public Tuesday to Saturday, 10.0–5.0; Sunday and Bank Holidays, 12.0–5.0; closed Mondays, Dec. 24–26, and 31, Jan. 1, and Good Friday.

Reference Library open by appointment.

Telephone 332900; website: www.fitzmuseum.cam.ac.uk

email: reception@fitzmuseum.cam.ac.uk

Director L. SYSON.

Museum of Archaeology and Anthropology

Open Tuesday to Saturday, 10.30–4.30 and Sunday, 12.0 to 4.30. Closed for approximately one week during Christmas/New Year, and on Good Friday and Easter Sunday.

Website: http://maa.cam.ac.uk

email: admin@maa.cam.ac.uk

Curator & Director, Prof. N. J. THOMAS.

Museum of Classical Archaeology

Cast gallery open to the public 10.0–5.0, Tuesday to Friday, Saturday 10.0–1.0. in Term time. (Closed Christmas, New Year, and Easter, and at the discretion of the authorities.)

Telephone, 330402; email, museum@classics.cam.ac.uk

Web: http://www.classics.cam.ac.uk/museum

Director, Y. GALANAKIS.

Zoology Museum

Admission is free and there is now a shop and café.

Open Tuesday-Saturday from 10 a.m. to 4.30 p.m. & Sunday from noon to 4.30 p.m. Last admission to the galleries is 4.0 p.m.

The Museum is closed on Mondays, Good Friday and during the Christmas/New Year period.

Telephone: 01223 336650

Email: umzc@cam.ac.uk

Web: www.museumofzoology.org.uk

Director, Prof. P.M. BRAKEFIELD.

The Polar Museum, Scott Polar Research Institute

Open Tuesday to Saturday, Good Friday, and public holiday Mondays, 10.0–4.0. Closed over the Christmas and New Year period. School parties by arrangement. Children must be accompanied by an adult. For further information telephone 336540.

Web: www.spri.cam.ac.uk

Director, Prof. J. A. DOWDESWELL.

Sedgwick Museum of Earth Sciences

The Museum is the oldest of the University museums and has a collection of more than two million items. All are welcome and entry is free.

Open Monday to Friday, 10.0–1.0, 2.0–5.0; Saturdays, 10.0–4.0.

Closed Good Friday.

Telephone 333456. *Email*: sedgwickmuseum@esc.cam .ac.uk

Web: http://www.sedgwickmuseum.org

Director, E. HIDE.

Whipple Museum of the History of Science

Open Monday to Friday from 12.30 to 4.30. The Museum is closed on public holidays and for a few days at Christmas and Easter. There are also occasional special events on selected evenings and weekends; please consult the website. For further information telephone 330906.

Web: http://www.hps.cam.ac.uk/whipple

Curator & Director, Prof. L. TAUB.

Botanic Garden

The Garden now holds more than 8000 plant species. Through the year it hosts events and courses announced on the website.

Admission and Opening Times (entry by Brookside and Station Road Gate).

January, November & December 10.0 a.m.–4.0 p.m.

February, March & October 10.0 a.m.–5.0 p.m.

April to September 10.0 a.m.–6.0 p.m.

An admission charge is made. Please note the Garden is closed from 24 December 2019 to 1 January 2020 inclusive.

Glasshouses and café close half an hour before Garden closing time. Shop closes 15 minutes before Garden closing time. Free admission to undergraduate and post-graduate students of the University upon production of a valid University Card. Last entry is 30 minutes before closing time.

Web: www.botanic.cam.ac.uk
Email: enquiries@botanic.cam.ac.uk
Telephone, 336265
Director, Prof. B. J. GLOVER.

Kettle's Yard, Castle Street

Kettle's Yard House displays modern art and hosts modern and contemporary exhibitions. The new building includes two galleries, a café, shop, welcome area, and a four-floor education wing. Admission is free.

Open Tuesday to Sunday from 11.a.m to 5 p.m.

For forthcoming events and exhibitions see kettlesyard.co.uk

ADC Theatre Park Street

The University playhouse. Two drama productions weekly (evenings) during Term and regular productions at other times.

Web: adctheatre.com; adcticketing.com

The ADC also manages the Corpus Playroom, an 80-seat venue in St Edward's Passage.

Administration, tel. 359547.
Booking, tel. 300085 and online.
Manager, V. J. COLLINS.

University Information Services J. J. Thomson Avenue

University Information Services provides IT, research computing and related services including networks, telephones, email, business systems, and a Service Desk for the University and its Colleges. For more information visit http://www.uis.cam.ac.uk/

Opening times for the UIS Reception and the Service Desk can found at

http://www.uis.cam.ac.uk/about-us/service-hours

Enquiries: reception@uis.cam.ac.uk

Director: Prof. I. M. LESLIE.

Telephone: 334600

University Language Centre Downing Place

The Centre promotes and supports language learning for personal, professional, and academic purposes. It offers taught courses for staff and students in a range of languages from absolute beginner to undergraduate level, English for Academic Purposes, support for international students, online and physical resources in over 180 languages, and a personalised advising service to support specific language learning goals. A University Card is required for registration. Non-members of the University may be offered limited access to resources for an annual fee.

The Language Centre is open Mon.–Fri. 9.30–7.30 in Full Term and during CULP teaching weeks, and 9.30–5.30 at other times.

Web: http://www.langcen.cam.ac.uk

Enquiries: enquiries@langcen.cam.ac.uk

Telephone: 335058

Director: J. WYBURD.

CAMBRIDGE UNIVERSITY STUDENTS' UNION

All students (undergraduate and postgraduates) automatically become members of CUSU when studying at Cambridge. CUSU represents and campaigns on behalf of its members, working hard to improve the student experience in all aspects of student life. Run by six elected officers (President, Education, Access, Welfare, Women's and Disabled), CUSU also provides a wide range of services and support, which includes the Print Shop, binding services, and facilitating the Clubs and Society Directory. Through the Students' Union Advice Service we are also able to offer confidential independent advice. CUSU welcomes engagement in its campaigns and encourages students to make contact if they would like to get involved, have any suggestions, or would like support of any kind.

CUSU's office, at 17 Mill Lane is open Monday – Friday, 9.0–5.0.

Telephone: 01223 333313
Email: reception@cusu.cam.ac.uk
Website: www.cusu.co.uk

GRADUATE UNION

The Graduate Union (GU) is the representative body for graduate students at the University of Cambridge. A democratic organisation, it is run by elected sabbatical officers & a board of elected student volunteers who focus on four key areas: representation, services, welfare, and events.

Officers take concerns raised by graduate students to a wide range of University committees, acting as the graduate student voice.

A wide range of facilities is offered at the centrally located premises: lounge, and shop, as well as such essential services as printing, binding, & gown hire. Rooms may be booked for meetings & events. The Students' Unions' Advice Service, run jointly by the GU & Cambridge University Students' Union, offers free, confidential, and independent support to all University of Cambridge students.

GU organises a wide range of activities and events during term and vacations. It publishes a free handbook & weekly bulletin, hosts an active forum, and offers many opportunities for graduate students to become involved.

Membership of the GU is free and automatic for graduate students and mature and fourth year undergraduates.

Address: 17 Mill Lane, Cambridge, CB2 1RX
Website: www.gradunion.cam.ac.uk
Email: enquiries@gradunion.cam.ac.uk
Telephone: 01223 333313
Open Monday to Friday: hours vary in and out of Term; see website for details.

NEWCOMERS & VISITING SCHOLARS

The University of Cambridge Newcomers and Visiting Scholars group welcomes newcomers (including post-docs, members of staff, and visiting scholars) and their families, and aims to make their stay in Cambridge enjoyable and successful. It provides a termly programme of events and various interest groups, e.g. book, film, culture, cookery and conversation groups. A meeting, usually with a speaker, is held every Tuesday in term time from 10.30 a.m. to 12.30 p.m. at the University Centre.

The group works closely with the Accommodation Service and Office of Postdoctoral Affairs.

See the website: http://www.nvs.admin.cam.ac.uk or email nvsadministrator@admin.cam.ac.uk for more information.

POSTDOCS OF CAMBRIDGE (PdOC)

Postdocs Of Cambridge is a society which aims to bring together postdoctoral research staff on both a social and an intellectual level and to improve their representation within Colleges and the University. It is open to all postdocs at the University and its Partner Institutions, and includes contract staff who have completed their doctorate but do not have long-term tenure or established positions. The society ensures that information about careers and professional development, college affiliation, and social and welfare provision, is widely disseminated.

Members meet for lunch every Tuesday at 1.15 p.m. in the Main Dining Hall of the University Centre, and on the last day of every month at 7 p.m in a Cambridge pub whose venue is published on the PdOC Society website. To join the mailing list see www.pdoc.cam.ac.uk

Email: pdoc@admin.cam.ac.uk

TEL: 01223 336741

UNIVERSITY CENTRE

The University Centre is a unique social space for university students, staff, alumni, and their guests. Within the building food can be found in the Main Dining Hall, Grads Cafe, and the Riverside Restaurant (Elior), while award winning wines can be found in the new CUC Wine Bar.

The University Centre, located on Granta Place overlooking the Cam, is more than just a place to eat : there are plenty of areas to relax, catch up on your emails, read the newspapers or study. Facilities at the University Centre include a widescreen TV, Blue Fitness suite, and a number of conference rooms. Lapwing wireless internet is available throughout the building, or members can alternatively obtain a wireless ticket from reception.

The Centre is open from 8a.m. to 11p.m. seven days a week. Further information may be obtained and bookings made as follows:

Main Reception 01223 337766
Conference Services 01223 337796
Email: Conferences@admin.cam.ac.uk
Riverside Restaurant (Elior) 01223 328559
Email: Riverside.Restaurant@elior.co.uk

UNIVERSITY COMBINATION ROOM

The Combination Room is for the use of current members and retired members of the Roll of the Regent House and their guests. Visiting academics may also be issued with access cards, on nomination by their College or Department.

The Combination Room is open Monday – Friday from 10a.m to 4p.m.

If you have any queries please email:
ReceptionOldSchools@admin.cam.ac.uk
Old Schools Reception: 01223 332200

DEVELOPMENT AND ALUMNI RELATIONS

The Development and Alumni Relations office is the alumni relations and fundraising arm of the University, responsible for raising major philanthropic gifts and building and sustaining lifelong links between Cambridge and its alumni and supporters across the globe.

Development and Alumni Relations is also responsible for principal alumni engagement programmes including the award-winning alumni magazine *CAM*, digital and e-communications and social media, and the annual Alumni Festival.

Find out about the range of benefits and services available to alumni and former postdocs online at www.alumni.cam.ac.uk and, for those in the USA and Canada, www.cantab.org.

Learn about the fundraising campaign for the University and Colleges at www.philanthropy.cam.ac.uk.

Contact us at:

University of Cambridge Development and Alumni Relations

1 Quayside, Bridge St, Cambridge, CB5 8AB, UK

Telephone, +44 (0)1223 332288

Email: contact@alumni.cam.ac.uk

contact@philanthropy.cam.ac.uk

Website, www.alumni.cam.ac.uk

www.philanthropy.cam.ac.uk

Cambridge in America

1120 Avenue of the Americas 17th Floor, New York, NY 10036, USA

Telephone, +1 212 984 0960

Email: mail@cantab.org

Website, www.cantab.org

COLLEGES, APPROVED
FOUNDATIONS, AND
APPROVED SOCIETIES

Christ's *Master*: Prof. J. STAPLETON. *Bursar*: D. BALL. *Senior Tutor*: R. HUNT.

Churchill *Master*: Prof. Dame Athene DONALD. *Bursar*: T. JAMES. *Senior Tutor*: R. J. PARTINGTON.

Clare *Master*: LORD GRABINER. *Bursar*: P. C. WARREN. *Senior Tutor*: J. A. TASIOULAS.

Clare Hall *President*: Prof. D. J. IBBETSON. *Bursar*: I. C. STRACHAN. *Senior Tutor*: I. S. BLACK.

Corpus Christi *Master*: Prof. C. M. KELLY. *Bursar*: T. J. HARVEY-SAMUEL. *Senior Tutor*: M. FRASCA-SPADA.

Darwin *Master*: Prof. C. M. R. FOWLER. *Bursar*: J. T. DIX. *Dean*: D. J. NEEDHAM.

Downing *Master*: A. P. BOOKBINDER. *Bursar*: S. E. LINTOTT. *Senior Tutor*: G. B. WILLIAMS.

Emmanuel *Master*: Dame Fiona REYNOLDS. *Bursar*: M. J. GROSS. *Senior Tutor*: R. M. HENDERSON.

Fitzwilliam *Master*: Lady MORGAN of HUYTON. *Bursar*: R. A. POWELL. *Senior Tutor*: P. A. CHIRICO.

Girton *Mistress*: Prof. S. J. SMITH. *Bursar*: D. LOWTHER. *Senior Tutor*: A. M. FULTON.

Gonville and Caius *Master*: P. J. ROGERSON. *Bursar*: R. GARDINER. *Senior Tutor*: A. M. SPENCER.

Homerton *Principal*: G. C. WARD. *Bursar*: D. GRIFFIN. *Senior Tutor*: P. BARTON.

Hughes Hall *President*: A. N. S. FREELING. *Bursar*: V. A. ESPLEY. *Senior Tutor*: P. JOHNSTON.

Jesus *Master*: S. ALLEYNE. *Bursar*: R. F. ANTHONY. *Senior Tutor*: G. T. PARKS.

King's *Provost*: Prof. M. R. E. PROCTOR. *Bursar*: T. K. CARNE. *Senior Tutor*: T. FLACK.

Lucy Cavendish *President*: Prof. Dame Madeleine ATKINS. *Bursar*: L. THOMPSON. *Senior Tutor*: J. GREATOREX.

Magdalene *Master*: Lord WILLIAMS OF OYSTERMOUTH. *Bursar*: S. J. MORRIS. *Senior Tutor*: S. MARTIN.

Murray Edwards *President*: Dame Barbara STOCKING. *Bursar*: R. HOPWOOD. *Senior Tutor*: K. PETERS.

Newnham *Principal*: A. ROSE. *Bursar*: C. LAWRENCE. *Tutor*: Prof. L. TAUB.

Pembroke *Master*: Lord SMITH OF FINSBURY. *Bursar*: A. T. CATES. *Senior Tutor*: A. W. TUCKER.

Peterhouse *Master*: B. KENDALL. *Bursar*: I. N. M. WRIGHT. *Senior Tutor*: S. W. P. HAMPTON.

Queens' *President*: Lord EATWELL. *Bursar*: J. SPENCE. *Senior Tutor*: J. W. KELLY.

Robinson *Warden*: A. D. YATES. *Finance Bursar*: F. BROCKBANK. *Senior Tutor*: D. A. WOODMAN.

St Catharine's *Master*: Prof. SIR MARK WELLAND. *Bursar*: N. ROBERT. *Senior Tutor*: M. H. GRIFFIN.

St Edmund's *Master*: C. E. J. ARNOLD. *Bursar*: E. MURPHY. *Senior Tutor*: J. M. BUNBURY.

St John's *Master*: Prof. Sir Christopher DOBSON. *Bursar*: C. F. EWBANK. *Senior Tutor*: A. M. TIMPSON.

Selwyn *Master*: R. MOSEY. *Bursar*: N. J. A. DOWNER. *Senior Tutor*: M. J. SEWELL.

Sidney Sussex *Master*: Prof. R. PENTY. *Bursar*: S. BONNETT. *Senior Tutor*: M. BEBER.

Trinity *Master*: Professor Dame Sally DAVIES. *Bursar*: R. LANDMAN. *Senior Tutor*: Prof. C. S. BARNARD.

Trinity Hall *Master*: J. N. MORRIS. *Bursar*: P. ffolkes DAVIS. *Senior Tutor*: J. C. JACKSON.

Wolfson *President*: Prof. J. CLARKE. *Bursar*: J. CHEFFINS. *Senior Tutor*: S. LARSEN.

COLLEGE INFORMATION

College websites have a great variety of information that is revised from time to time. Typically they include details of admission, Fellows and staff, alumni, maps, libraries and chapels, current events, historical notes, photographs, societies, and a means of searching the whole archive for specific topics. Colleges also have entries in the online undergraduate and graduate studies prospectuses.

Addresses, all of which follow the standard 'http://www.', and do not admit apostrophes (e.g. Christ's = http://www.christs.cam.ac.uk/) are these:

Christ's	christs.cam.ac.uk
Churchill	chu.cam.ac.uk
Clare	clare.cam.ac.uk
Clare Hall	clarehall.cam.ac.uk
Corpus Christi	corpus.cam.ac.uk
Darwin	dar.cam.ac.uk
Downing	dow.cam.ac.uk
Emmanuel	emma.cam.ac.uk
Fitzwilliam	fitz.cam.ac.uk
Girton	girton.cam.ac.uk
Gonville & Caius	cai.cam.ac.uk
Homerton	homerton.cam.ac.uk
Hughes Hall	hughes.cam.ac.uk
Jesus	jesus.cam.ac.uk
King's	kings.cam.ac.uk
Lucy Cavendish	lucy-cav.cam.ac.uk
Magdalene	magd.cam.ac.uk
Murray Edwards	murrayedwards.cam.ac.uk
Newnham	newn.cam.ac.uk
Pembroke	pem.cam.ac.uk
Peterhouse	pet.cam.ac.uk
Queens'	queens.cam.ac.uk
Robinson	robinson.cam.ac.uk
St Catharine's	caths.cam.ac.uk

St Edmund's	st-edmunds.cam.ac.uk
St John's	joh.cam.ac.uk
Selwyn	sel.cam.ac.uk
Sidney Sussex	sid.cam.ac.uk
Trinity	trin.cam.ac.uk
Trinity Hall	trinhall.cam.ac.uk
Wolfson	wolfson.cam.ac.uk

MOVABLE FEASTS

	2019–2020	2020–2021
1st Sunday in Advent	Dec. 1	Nov. 29
Ash Wednesday	Feb. 26	Feb. 17
Easter Day	Apr. 12	Apr. 4
Ascension Day	May 21	May 13
Whitsunday	May 31	May 23
Trinity Sunday	June 7	May 30
Corpus Christi	June 11	June 3

A list of movable feasts to the year 2035 may be found in *Whitaker's Almanack*, together with full calendars for the years 1780–2040.

FULL TERMS

2019–2020
Michaelmas: Oct. 8–Dec. 6
Lent: Jan. 14–Mar. 13
Easter: Apr. 21–June 12

2020–2021
Michaelmas: Oct. 6–Dec. 4
Lent: Jan. 19–Mar. 19
Easter: Apr. 27–June 18

2021–2022
Michaelmas: Oct. 5–Dec. 3
Lent: Jan. 18–Mar. 18
Easter: Apr. 26–June 17

2022–2023
Michaelmas: Oct. 4–Dec. 2
Lent: Jan. 17–Mar. 17
Easter: Apr. 25–June 16

For later dates see the current edition of *Statutes & Ordinances*.

Michaelmas Term begins on Oct. 1 and ends on Dec. 19. Lent Term begins on Jan. 5 and ends on Mar. 25 (or 24 in any leap year, the next being 2020). Easter Term begins on Apr. 10 and ends on June 18, but falls a week *later* whenever Full Easter Term begins on or after Apr. 22, as in the years 2019–2030 inclusive, except for 2020.

THE RIVER

Order of Boats in the Main Divisions, 2019

LENTS

Men's Division 1

1	(2)	CAI 1	10	(13)	TH 1
2	(1)	LMBC 1	11	(8)	PET 1
3	(3)	DOW 1	12	(17)	K 1
4	(4)	PEM 1	13	(9)	CL 1
5	(7)	R 1	14	(16)	M 1
6	(5)	JE 1	15	(18)	EM 1
7	(10)	1&3T 1	16	(12)	Q 1
8	(11)	CTH 1	17	(19)	F 1
9	(6)	CHR 1			

Women's Division 1

1	(3)	N 1	10	(8)	CHR 1
2	(1)	JE 1	11	(12)	CHU 1
3	(5)	EM 1	12	(6)	ME 1
4	(2)	DOW 1	13	(16)	CAI 1
5	(9)	LMBC 1	14	(11)	G 1
6	(7)	1&3T 1	15	(19)	F 1
7	(10)	PEM 1	16	(14)	CTH 1
8	(4)	CL 1	17	(15)	Q 1
9	(13)	TH 1			

Numbers in brackets show position of boats at start of races.

MAYS

Men's Division 1

1	(4)	*CAI* 1	10	(12)	*K* 1
2	(5)	*M* 1	11	(13)	*R* 1
3	(1)	*LMBC* 1	12	(9)	*JE* 1
4	(6)	*DOW* 1	13	(17)	*LMBC* 2
5	(7)	*EM* 1	14	(11)	*Q* 1
6	(3)	*PEM* 1	15	(14)	*CHR* 1
7	(10)	*PET* 1	16	(21)	*TH* 1
8	(2)	*CL* 1	17	(15)	*SE* 1
9	(8)	*1&3T* 1			

Women's Division 1

1	(2)	*N* 1	10	(6)	*CL* 1
2	(1)	*JE* 1	11	(13)	*F* 1
3	(3)	*EM* 1	12	(8)	*G* 1
4	(5)	*CAI* 1	13	(12)	*CHR* 1
5	(7)	*LMBC* 1	14	(17)	*Q* 1
6	(4)	*DOW* 1	15	(16)	*CTH* 1
7	(11)	*PEM* 1	16	(18)	*TH* 1
8	(9)	*CHU* 1	17	(14)	*HO* 1
9	(10)	*1&3T* 1			

Numbers in brackets show position of boats at start of races.

INTER-UNIVERSITY CONTESTS,
2018–2019

Based on information supplied in mid-June

Men's Matches

Association Football	Cambridge
Athletics (indoor)	Oxford
Athletics (outdoor)	Oxford
Badminton	Cambridge
Basketball	Cambridge
Boat Race	Cambridge
Boxing	Cambridge
Canoe Marathon	
Canoe Polo	
Cricket (1 day)	Oxford
Cricket (2020)	Cambridge
Cross Country	Oxford
Cycling (MTB)	Cambridge
Cycling (road)	Cambridge
Duathlon	Oxford
Fencing	Oxford
Fives (Eton)	Oxford
Fives (Rugby)	Oxford
Golf	Oxford
Gymnastics	Cambridge
Handball	Cambridge
Hockey	Cambridge
Ice Hockey	Cambridge
Judo	Oxford
Karate	Cambridge
Lacrosse	Oxford
Lightweight Rowing	Oxford
Modern Pentathlon	Cambridge
Orienteering	Oxford
Pistol	
Polo	
Real Tennis	Oxford
Rifle Shooting	Oxford
Rugby League	
Rugby Union	Oxford
Ski & Snowboard	Oxford

Squash	Oxford
Swimming	Cambridge
Table Tennis	Cambridge
Triathlon	Oxford
Ultimate Frisbee	Oxford
Volleyball	Oxford
Water Polo	Cambridge

Women's Matches

Association Football	Cambridge
Athletics	Oxford
Badminton	Oxford
Basketball	
Boat Race	Cambridge
Canoe Marathon	
Canoe Polo	
Cricket (2020)	Oxford
Cross Country	Cambridge
Cycling (MTB)	
Cycling (Road)	Oxford
Duathlon	Cambridge
Fives (Eton)	Oxford
Fives (Rugby)	Cambridge
Golf	Oxford
Gymnastics	Cambridge
Handball	Oxford
Hockey	Oxford
Ice Hockey	Cambridge
Judo	Cambridge
Karate	Oxford
Lacrosse	Cambridge
Lightweight Rowing	Oxford
Modern Pentathlon	Cambridge
Netball	Oxford
Orienteering	Cambridge
Pistol	
Polo	Cambridge
Real Tennis	Oxford
Rifle Shooting	
Rugby Union	Cambridge
Ski & Snowboard	Cambridge

Squash	Cambridge
Swimming	Oxford
Table Tennis	Cambridge
Triathlon	Oxford
Ultimate Frisbee (indoor)	Cambridge
Ultimate Frisbee (outdoor)	Oxford
Volleyball	Oxford
Water Polo	Oxford

Mixed Teams

American Football	Oxford
Archery	Oxford
Athletics (outdoor)	
Dancesport	Cambridge
Gliding	Cambridge
Karate	
Korfball	Oxford
Lacrosse	Cambridge
Powerlifting	Cambridge
Riding	
Small Bore	
Trampoline	Oxford
Ultimate Frisbee (indoor)	Cambridge
Ultimate Frisbee (outdoor)	Cambridge
Yachting	Cambridge

LONDON TRAINS

The frequency of London trains, and of alterations especially at weekends, make it inadvisable to print the timetables, but space has been left on the following page to enter details. The service may be amended in the course of the academical year.

Trains on the London routes are operated by different companies under contracts which change from time to time. The faster and more frequent services run to and from King's Cross, and there are slower trains to and from Liverpool Street. Some trains on the King's Cross route now run across London to Gatwick airport and the south coast, calling at St Pancras International station. The best source of timetable and other information is by accessing the National Rail Enquiries website:

http://www.nationalrail.co.uk, or by telephoning 0345748 49 50.

Cambridge North station will be convenient for passengers in the north of the city, including the Science Park. There are services to and from King's Cross, Liverpool Street, King's Lynn, and Norwich.

It is important to check train times at weekends and public holidays: details of forthcoming alterations are available from National Rail Enquiries.

There are also regular train services to Peterborough (for the East Coast main line), Norwich, Ipswich, Stansted Airport, and the Midlands.

June 2019

LONDON TRAINS

(see note on p. 321)

COACHES

Cambridge to Oxford & to London Airports
from Cambridge, Drummer Street/Parkside

All services are frequent throughout the day, as are return services.

For further information please use the following contact numbers and websites, which also give access to other destinations, etc.*

National Express: tel. 08717 818181
　　　　Website – www.nationalexpress.com

Oxford

Via St Neots, Bedford, Milton Keynes, Buckingham, and Bicester

Stagecoach Bus: tel. 01234 220030
　　　　Website – www.stagecoachx5.com

London Airports

National Express runs coaches from Parkside to Stansted and Luton, and to Heathrow (all terminals) and Gatwick.

National Express also operates an express service to London Victoria Coach Station; it takes about two hours.

* Correct at 9 June

TELEPHONE NUMBERS

The STD code for Cambridge is 01223, prefixed by + 44 from abroad.

University Network

The University Telephone Network is an internal system linking Departments and Colleges. There is a central switchboard (337733) and numbers for most extensions are five digit numbers. Network directories are no longer available, but see

www.cam.ac.uk/email-and-phone-search

Please use the online https://www.lookup.cam.ac.uk

Most extensions are 33xxxx; others are 74xxxx and 76xxxx.

Access codes are still needed for these destinations:

Addenbrooke's Hospital 700
Med. Res. Council (LMB) 145

University Departments, etc.

332200	Academic Division
338099	Accommodation Service
334396	African Studies Centre
356942	Air Squadron
217889	Anaesthesia, Division of
335079	Anglo-Saxon, Norse, & Celtic, Dept. of
765000	Applied Mathematics and Theoretical Physics, Dept. of
765040	Applied Research in Educational Technologies, Centre for (CARET)
333538	Archaeology Dept. of
333516	Arch. and Anth., Museum of
332950	Architecture, Dept. of
333147 } 333148	Archives
766222	Arts & Humanities, School of
766886	Arts, Social Sciences & Humanities, Research Centre for

Colleges
With postcodes

334900	Christ's CB2 3BU
336000	Churchill CB3 0DS
333200	Clare CB2 1TL
332360	Clare Hall CB3 9AL
338000	Corpus Christi CB2 1RH
335660	Darwin CB3 9EU
334800	Downing CB2 1DQ
334200	Emmanuel CB2 3AP
332000	Fitzwilliam CB3 0DG
338999	Girton CB3 0JG
332400	Gonville and Caius CB2 1TA
747111	Homerton CB2 8PH
334898	Hughes Hall CB1 2EW
339339	Jesus CB5 8BL
331100	King's CB2 1ST
332190	Lucy Cavendish CB3 0BU
332100	Magdalene CB3 0AG
762100	Murray Edwards CB3 0DF
335700	Newnham CB3 9DF
338100	Pembroke CB2 1RF
338200	Peterhouse CB2 1RD
335511	Queens' CB3 9ET
339100	Robinson CB3 9AN
332300	St Catharine's CB2 1RL
336250	St Edmund's CB3 0BN
338600	St John's CB2 1TP
335846	Selwyn CB3 9DQ
338800	Sidney Sussex CB2 3HU
338400	Trinity CB2 1TQ
332500	Trinity Hall CB2 1TJ
335900	Wolfson CB3 9BB

Miscellaneous

359547	ADC Theatre
245151	Addenbrooke's Hospital, General Enquiries
217118	Accident & Emergency
01245 493131	Anglia Ruskin University
496000	Babraham Institute
741251	Blackfriars
221400	British Antarctic Survey
457000	Cambridge City Council
101	Cambridge City Police
767787	Cambridge Theological Federation
706050	Cambridge Water Company (day and night)
768740	Conference Cambridge
311545	East Asian History of Science Library (Needham Research Institute)
742192	Fisher House
315084	Joint Colleges Nursery Linkline
267000	Molecular Biology (M.R.C. Laboratory)
342200	Nat. Inst. of Agric. Botany (NIAB)
744444	Nightline
303336	Nuffield Hospital
361851	Open University
0845 7484950	Railway Inquiries
245888	Rape Crisis Centre, Cambridge
746580	Ridley Hall
364455	Samaritans, Cambridge
350365	Student Community Action
337575	Varsity Newspaper
765832	Wesley House
741000	Westcott House
330633	Westminster College

Fax, Email & Websites

Various directories may be searched on the Web (see below). The following fax numbers may be found especially useful:

334679	Information Services
765094	Finance Division
332277	Academic Division
332322	Registrary's Office
333160	University Library
315052	University Press

World Wide Web

For Colleges see pp. 313–14.

The URL of the University Web server is http://www.cam.ac.uk/. This has links to Departmental, College, and other specialised servers. Some useful links are:

University web search: http://search.cam.ac.uk
Email & phone search (including University-only search):
  http://www.cam.ac.uk/email-and-phone-search
University Map:
  http://www.cam.ac.uk/map
University Telecoms Office:
  http://phone.cam.ac.uk
University Reporter:
  http://www.admin.cam.ac.uk/reporter
Statutes & Ordinances:
  http://www.admin.cam.ac.uk/univ/so
University Library: http://www.lib.cam.ac.uk
University Offices: http://www.admin.cam.ac.uk
University Information Services: http://www.uis.cam.ac.uk
Other servers in the University:
  http://www.cam.ac.uk/university-a-z

MAYOR OF LONDON